B40

2/A

257

Pebble®
Bilingüe/
Bilingual Plus

¿QUÉ HAY EN MiPlato?

LÁCTEOS
en MiPlato

WHAT'S ON MyPlate?

DAIRY
on MyPlate

por/by Mari Schuh

Editora consultora/Consulting Editor:
Gail Saunders-Smith, PhD

Consultora/Consultant: Barbara J. Rolls, PhD
Guthrie Chair en Nutrición/Guthrie Chair in Nutrition
Pennsylvania State University
University Park, Pennsylvania

CAPSTONE PRESS
a capstone imprint

Pebble Plus is published by Capstone Press,
1710 Roe Crest Drive, North Mankato, Minnesota 56003
www.capstonepub.com

Library of Congress Cataloging-in-Publication Data
Schuh, Mari C., 1975–
   Lácteos en miplato = Dairy on myplate / por Mari Schuh ; editora consultora, Gail Saunders-Smith, PhD.
      pages cm. — (Pebble plus bilingüe. ¿Qué hay en miplato? = Pebble plus bilingual. What's on myplate?)
   Spanish and English.
   Includes index.
   ISBN 978-1-62065-941-0 (library binding)
   ISBN 978-1-4765-1763-6 (ebook PDF)
   1. Dairy products—Juvenile literature. 2. Dairy products in human nutrition—Juvenile literature. I. Saunders-
Smith, Gail, editor. II. Schuh, Mari C., 1975– Dairy on myplate. Spanish. III. Schuh, Mari C., 1975– Dairy on
myplate. IV. Title. V. Title: Dairy on myplate. VI. Title: Lácteos en miplato. VII. Title: Dairy on myplate.
TX377.S37818 2013
641.6'7—dc23   2012023315

Summary: Simple text and photos describe USDA's MyPlate tool and healthy dairy choices for
children—in both English and Spanish

Editorial Credits
Jeni Wittrock, editor; Strictly Spanish, translation services; Gene Bentdahl, designer; Eric Manske, bilingual book
designer; Svetlana Zhurkin, media researcher; Jennifer Walker, production specialist; Sarah Schuette, photo stylist;
Marcy Morin, studio scheduler

Photo Credits
All photos by Capstone Studio/Karon Dubke except:
Shutterstock: Magone, cover (bottom), manaemedia, back cover, Melica, cover (top right); USDA, cover (inset), 5

The author dedicates this book to her niece, Camryn Schuh of Mankato, Minnesota.

Information in this book supports
the U.S. Department of Agriculture's
MyPlate food guidance system found at
www.choosemyplate.gov. Food amounts
listed in this book are based on daily
recommendations for children ages 4-8.
The amounts listed in this book are
appropriate for children who get less than
30 minutes a day of moderate physical
activity, beyond normal daily activities.
Children who are more physically active
may be able to eat more while staying
within calorie needs. The U.S. Department
of Agriculture (USDA) does not endorse
any products, services, or organizations.

Note to Parents and Teachers

The ¿Qué hay en MiPlato?/What's on MyPlate? series supports national science standards
related to health and nutrition. This book describes and illustrates MyPlate's dairy
recommendations. The images support early readers in understanding the text. The repetition of
words and phrases helps early readers learn new words. This book also introduces early readers
to subject-specific vocabulary words, which are defined in the Glossary section. Early readers
may need assistance to read some words and to use the Table of Contents, Glossary, Internet
Sites, and Index sections of the book.

Printed in China.
092012   006934LEOS13

Table of Contents

MyPlate 4

Dairy Foods 6

Enjoying the Dairy Group 12

How Much to Eat 20

Glossary 22

Internet Sites 22

Index 24

Tabla de contenidos

MiPlato 4

Alimentos lácteos 6

Disfruta el grupo lácteo 12

Cuánto comer 20

Glosario 23

Sitios de Internet 23

Índice 24

MyPlate/ MiPlato

The dairy group is a tasty part of MyPlate. MyPlate is a tool that helps you eat healthful food.

El grupo lácteo es una parte muy rica de MiPlato. MiPlato es una herramienta que te ayuda a comer alimentos saludables.

4

Fruits/
Frutas

Grains/
Granos

Dairy/
Lácteos

Vegetables/
Vegetales

Protein/
Proteína

MiPlato
Choose**MyPlate**.gov

Dairy Foods/ Alimentos lácteos

Milk, cheese, and yogurt are part
of the dairy group.
Have you eaten dairy foods today?

La leche, el queso y el yogur son parte
del grupo lácteo.
¿Has comido alimentos lácteos hoy?

Dairy foods have calcium.
Your bones and teeth need calcium
to grow healthy and strong.

Los alimentos lácteos tienen calcio.
Tus huesos y dientes necesitan calcio para
crecer fuertes y saludables.

Kids ages 4 to 8 should eat and drink 2½ cups (600 milliliters) from the dairy group every day.

Los niños entre 4 y 8 años deberían comer y beber 2½ tazas (600 mililitros) del grupo lácteo cada día.

Enjoying the Dairy Group/ Disfruta el grupo lácteo

Different kinds of milk have different amounts of fat.
Choose low-fat milk.
It's better for you.

Diferentes tipos de leche tienen diferentes cantidades de grasa.
Selecciona leche baja en grasas.
Es mejor para ti.

13

Cheese can be hard, soft,
yellow, or white.
An adult can help you read
the labels to choose low-fat cheese.

El queso puede ser duro, blando,
amarillo o blanco.
Un adulto puede ayudarte a leer las etiquetas
para seleccionar queso bajo en grasas.

Dairy foods taste great with other foods.
For a sweet snack, add fruit to your
creamy yogurt.

Los alimentos lácteos son muy ricos
con otros alimentos.
Para una merienda dulce, agrega
fruta a tu yogur cremoso.

Add low-fat yogurt
to your baked potato.
Sprinkle low-fat cheese
on a bowl of soup.

Agrega yogur bajo en grasas
a tu papa al horno.
Rocía queso bajo en grasas
a un tazón de sopa.

How Much to Eat/ Cuánto comer

Most kids need to have three servings from the dairy group every day. Pick three of your favorite dairy products to enjoy today!

La mayoría de los niños necesitan comer tres porciones del grupo lácteo todos los días. ¡Selecciona tres de tus alimentos lácteos favoritos para disfrutar hoy!

2 ounces (55 grams) processed cheese

2 onzas (55 gramos) de queso procesado

⅓ cup (80 mL) shredded cheese

⅓ taza (80 ml) de queso rallado

1 cup (240 mL) yogurt

1 taza (240 ml) de yogur

1 cup (240 mL) fat-free milk

1 taza (240 ml) de leche sin grasa

1 cup (240 mL) soymilk

1 taza (240 ml) de leche de soja

1½ ounces (45 grams) hard cheeses

1½ onzas (45 gramos) de queso duro

2 cups (480 mL) cottage cheese

2 tazas (480 ml) de queso cottage

1 cup (240 mL) pudding made with milk

1 taza (240 ml) de pudding hecho con leche

Glossary

calcium—a mineral that the body uses to build teeth and bones

dairy—foods that are made with milk; milk, cheese, and yogurt are kinds of dairy foods

low-fat—containing a small amount of fat; dairy foods that are low-fat are better for you than dairy foods with more fat

MyPlate—a food plan that reminds people to eat healthful food and be active; MyPlate was created by the U.S. Department of Agriculture

serving—one helping of food

Internet Sites

FactHound offers a safe, fun way to find Internet sites related to this book. All of the sites on FactHound have been researched by our staff.

Here's all you do:

Visit *www.facthound.com*

Type in this code: 9781620659410

Check out projects, games and lots more at
www.capstonekids.com

Glosario

bajo en grasas—que contiene poca cantidad de grasas; los alimentos lácteos que son bajos en grasas son mejores para ti que los alimentos lácteos con más grasa

el calcio—un mineral que el cuerpo usa para fortalecer los dientes y huesos

los lácteos—alimentos hechos con leche; leche, queso y yogur son tipos de alimentos lácteos

MiPlato—un plan de alimentos que hace recordar a la gente de comer alimentos saludables y de estar activos; MiPlato fue creado por el Departamento de Agricultura de EE.UU.

la porción—una ración de alimento

Sitios de Internet

FactHound brinda una forma segura y divertida de encontrar sitios de Internet relacionados con este libro. Todos los sitios en FactHound han sido investigados por nuestro personal.

Esto es todo lo que tienes que hacer:

Visita *www.facthound.com*

Ingresa este código: 9781620659410

Hay proyectos, juegos y mucho más en
www.capstonekids.com

23

Index

calcium, 8

cheese, 6, 14, 18

labels, 14

low fat, 12, 14, 18

milk, 6, 12

MyPlate, 4

servings, 10, 20

yogurt, 6, 16, 18

Índice

bajo en grasas, 12, 14, 18

calcio, 8

etiquetas, 14

leche, 6, 12

MiPlato, 4

porciones, 10, 20

queso, 6, 14, 18

yogur, 6, 16, 18